Goners

KRISTI MAXWELL
WINNER OF THE WISHING JEWEL PRIZE

Green Linden Press
208 Broad Street South
Grinnell, Iowa 50112
www.greenlindenpress.com

First printing, 2023
Printed on recycled paper in the United States of America

Library of Congress Cataloging-in-Publication Data

Names: Maxwell, Kristi, author.
Title: Goners / Kristi Maxwell.
Description: Grinnell, Iowa : Green Linden Press, 2023. | Series: The Wishing Jewel Prize
Identifiers: LCCN 2023031960 | ISBN 9781961834989 (paperback)
Subjects: LCGFT: Experimental poetry.
Classification: LCC PS3613.A916 G66 2023 | DDC 811/.6—dc23/eng/20230717
LC record available at https://lccn.loc.gov/2023031960

Cover photo: *Ammonites* (Adobe Stock)
Book design: Christopher Nelson

Green Linden Press is a nonprofit publisher dedicated to fostering excellent poetry and
supporting reforestation with a portion of proceeds.

for once

Contents

"apricot trees exist, apricot trees exist"
—Inger Christensen, trans. Susanna Nied

"and so we live, constantly saying farewell"
—Rainer Maria Rilke, trans. Alfred Corn

EXTINCTION IS A PROBLEM OF FORM: A NOTE ON PROCESS

In *The New Poetics of Climate Change,* Matthew Griffiths asks, "Must poetry of climate change belong in the tradition of the pastoral or the elegy? … What alternative models or approaches might there be?" *Goners* explores some alternatives.

These poems are lipograms, writing that excludes one or more letters. They take as their starting place the names of endangered species and emerged out of a desire to manage my own climate despair. Specifically, I'm working with a variation of the beautiful outlaw—lipograms that do not use the letters in the title, the name of the endangered species, a variation I've come to call an extinction—to explore what happens when what is endangered is instead absent—gone. The piece "Cheetah," for instance, uses 21 of 26 letters, all but "a," "c," "e," "h," and "t," so no articles, no *cats*, no *being*, no *are* or *were* or *was*, no *choice*, etc. (no *etc.*). The formal strategy of the lipogram nods to global trends regarding climate change and strategies of elimination (eliminating carbon emissions, red meat consumption, plastic). When I first began sharing drafts of these poems with my writing group, they kept asking, "But where's the animal?," expecting the species in the individual poem titles to be reflected upon in the body of the poems. Instead, the pieces tend to be human-centered, a gesture I at first resisted, but then gave into because it seems to foreground the role human-centering has played and continues to play in the sixth extinction underway.

What I stress now: I'm not writing *about* endangered species; I'm writing *without* them—attempting to imagine in a linguistic landscape the ways that loss would be registered and felt or fail to be. The manuscript in general operates with the belief extinction is a problem of form, and I hope to think beyond extinctions of species, i.e., non-human animal erasures. I'm thinking of genocides and the corrosive effects of imperialism and industrialization, but also of the glaciers' melt as an erasure, deforestation as erasure, ocean acidification as at least a bad revision in which the wrong things have been added in and edited out.

Building off of Anna Lowenhaupt Tsing's language from *The Mushroom at the End of the World: On the Possibility of Life in Capitalist Ruins,* I've come to think of the lipogram as an "art of living on a damaged planet." As a formal strategy, and in thinking of the English language as a metonym for Western hegemony, the lipogram seems like a play on or performance of "capitalist ruins," a record of the fallout, centered on erosive energies. Perhaps the lipogram is an experiment in "ruining" language (all the while reveling in its resilience)—stunting the relationship between mastery and writing—and creating compositional events in which we're asked to consider what's at stake in being made to slow down and what happens when we put sugar in the tank of language, "raging against the machine." Perhaps the lipogram is a revolt.

I've come to call the poems in this manuscript my demented ark, playing, too, on the homophone *arc* and the idea of a broken trajectory. Each piece has a "companion piece," meaning, there are two poems generated for each endangered animal that appears in the collection, playing on the story of the Ark and founding mythologies about human intervention and preservation bound up in it.

Goners

DIBATAG

an extinction

welcome, wholesome voyeurs—
Lowell's-skunk wholesome, empresses of crème,
who prefer sour over funky or choose lower volumes
for love's solos (love commonly over-performs)

here, envy mooches off chlorophyll's work,
sponsors chlorophyll's one-sun show (essence: chlorophyll hoovers
specks of sun plus resourcefully reuses—surely, our clumsy folklore

ensorcells)—see cooks fume over flourless roux ("no such slurry!") (self's own slur)

when ozone chokes up, we console—
over here's our mock-up of numen
for our new elsewhere
where scenes of men show no cloven hooves

keep up: even foyers where we queue look lonesome
loosen now your peels, unlock your sunken forms

'Akeke'e
an extinction

Thought sumptuous   this skin thought "hungry gown"
mouthing off to its own dough   this youthful body

  silo-still   impounding storms

   scrubbing stupidity off this truly bright moon

Bluntly put: this body is Q-tip's trough   dip in

Critics flinch, but

  Food isn't just for mouths

   Light is photo's grub
    innocuous potion

  Slough off this "triumph" notion

Wood should not rot but it rots

   Sorry to limbs, sorry to gibbons
  sorry to hobos bound not to find
    North or South
     old stops
     thorough or not

This jinx is rough
Flimsy quiz: *how to undo it?*

If now word upon word is wordsmith's tumor
If now blight is ousting frost

        How to proctor un-birth?
How to win this Loss Bowl with history's surplus
        of wind-trysting birds
      blinding us from punting through the posts?

Cui-ui
an extinction

flesh-forward to now   my harlot remnant opposed the haggle

maybe gastronomy gave more to the world than gene therapy   overall

(my lament: sponsored by my damages   a story on wellness's edge

forgotten as a globe   the aloha ghost long ago harmed by a voyager)

we gave the sea a sampler of flotsam   the sea preferred none of what we gave

bon voyage, dear anthropomorph   the fever, like an earth, has thawed

the onlooker weans her own eyes off the handsome loam

the go-between between growth and harvest   the besotted spore

how have we gone from agro- to aggro   from leaf to leaflet

the pamphleteer hankers for new goals and for more paper, fresh as wet blood

CHEETAH
an extinction

my folks sold moon-yolk, forks of limp sun
no pow, so sulky bombs, no ping, so surly guns, no jig, so forlorn proms
my mood is missing, my limbs no rooms for birds
your SUV runs on skim milk, syrup, piss, mows down droopy blooms,
mills silky wounds in woods—giddy-up, womb, sing slow-mo vows
for girls, boys, ponds of gold lox, blond minnows, pounds of bling, sing
sorry for killing wings, for killing floors your mop lulls—

spill: living is frigid wound or sloppy diss? Sound off: grim voids, go on,
un-loop   Jury of punks, of fools, growl "boo" or lip "no sin found"
look: sub *grin* for *grim*, usurp glib dominions,
prowl pro-prowl soil   Fond of food, you pork pigs   poof!
poor pigs in your body's slum   sniff, sniff   found, pro-
found   Lungs unfold   grow
        You: born proud, pom-poms up

lump sum or dim sum, win now or nil
I is form   is us-plug   is solo fling   is void or ibis
is lol   poor film, minus wow, missing swigs of rum, pours of gin, only:
moss woos rock, would woos will, pus woos oozy   *fin*
        Is grim   fins of wood spook us, rob our lord's mind
sumo king of sulk, bow down   no wig will un-spy you
your own billowing I bills you for us-ing   for I's division

KOALA
an extinction

different fires require different fixes
wetness isn't it every time

did Muir grieve missing species' preceding densities—
see their missingness   the edges' misgivings

perceive the un-
quinces didn't preserve

residues extend remembering—the tide
venturing in, the drying spume
its spine   the spirit vein deveined   deemed excess

we experienced judgment when wind whipped us

meted mischief by describing—
fruit is a tree's sequins

ruined by the bite
who isn't though

(get even, Eve)

is this triggering
this being minted by suffering

the minute (but this isn't time—try twice) the minute
the determining mini

teensy thing   *the seeming*

MUSK DEER
an extinction

atop, bonito flit, bonito clown   a haint-colony
      biota of YOLO

          canola oil, too, acting living by popping

    a pool into which gill, tail, gill, tail   fall

        blot that glow

caption that: *if pain cannot notify it of pain*
        lob off! filch!   a clot in a bowl

       no long bloat

    a colonic plow got going that lava
       that galloping loot   (whiff)
              (woof)

       clog *all* with *any*

a twilight cannot want a vacation
a path of totality cannot want half

    to want to call holy
a typical fawn in a typical lawn bowing in a typical way
            intact

Cui-ui
an extinction

Drool grows to flood. Not a handsome wet.

Forget blood's fleet. Forget bloom's flop. A woman leaks. Forget grass

as green's poster-kid. One fawns over a doe. One yawns and a yodel

emerges. Address a meadow as land's slow jam.

    Groove. A bone

        hardly stops a beastly storm. Fog as a plaster

        on the broken sky. Hope softens. A flagrant web of hope

        passes as home, morphs to table. We're the meal.

        Even so, today, the holster hosts no weapon,

        not even a fang.

TOTOABA

an extinction

in reminiscence, we fissure   wish we'd
given pin-up girls sleeves   un-mused skins, given us
kinder windshields   enduring sunrise-less skies

even if I were kelp-useful   I deserve
my shushing   my grief is niche   princely
-ish—drinks my sluicing veil   my milklessness

we're likely rudders   unhinged   yet, when driven, impressive

eliding dependence, we're ellipses—wieldier puncs

I'll snuggle my newlywed mercy   I'll suckle my hex
heed cells whispering   *defense, defense*
implied   *wink, wink*—   we yell   *uncle*

we yell   *niece*   my finder's keeper is firm
I need find my skulking dirge   see if simile indeed frees

shedding my shed   cues the shivering

GIBBON
an extinction

the last lake suffers
yet we eschew the pharmacy
quash each thermal mystery
jadedly call a caldera a structural carcass
purse at sympathy's aftertaste

the marquee reads: rescue the plural
remake the remake   remake us   them

*

the camera pursued space stuff

flashy spheres

          a dream's caesura

               fake thyme   a flawed drawl

we read swelter's sweat-essay   faced the rheumy fact

     we had utterly wasted water   what else

Serow
an extinction

animalizing a day by giving it a hump   a day aping land   an aging hill

humanizing a villain by handing him vital liquid   actually bidding him, "maintain"

liquidating light   a blacklight making appalling an agitating fact   hacking it

pinching   data's flab   a fallacy   a lullaby failing to lull

calamity—haughty kin that ixnay making annual a unifying

kin that gladly milk that humanity gland   a tacky caulk

aiding a damming   filling a fault in an adult   a guilt

but a happy vault   habitual pillaging built up

cannibalizing any living thing   lack-binging

Xanadu: a dividing habitat   a gill-blank halibut   a half-fib

SEROW
an extinction

Again, that caftan-clad ninja did magnify panic, did publicly hunt public guilt

Again, my idling id did hack up that giddy lava, my un-I, lactating pulpy pudding, liquid *lingua*—talk, again   plug my gap   again, again

        pita-built, having amply an inn
        in my gut

          I'll gulp
              I'll gulf that I may fill

            I'm panhandling in a tidal-aching night

        a humpback dialing up land

          talk

  amid damaging lack   khaki-dull

    amid gag-inducing   milky light

      again, nudging

      again, guiding magic

      away

GAVIAL
an extinction

Someone deforested the moment to mourn

To quote the keeper: power to the odorous fester

Stumped by horror's modesty

The best snout wedded to the worst scent

The queen heron offers the "S"   her own neck for our words

Honesty fosters freedom

Frost knotted under snow   (nodded under snow)

Ponds ponder the wet moon, the herb orb the sheen stocks

Preference exerts pressure to reject   when one need not

There's rumor of tomorrow

Stunt of un-deep depth   humored, meme to meme

Not rejected-weed hurt, but on course

OKAPI
an extinction

un—verse, un—verse   hurt clusters, sewn—sutured

we were the end's veneers, yet even the end deserted us

chewed by nettles, deterred by reeds, we relented

we were the merest museum we'd ever shuttered

the smuggest event-less venue

sweet segments were squeezed, but we were unquenched

newly geysered, curfew blew

cement—the newer flesh—crumbled

meters were fed, but we weren't

Everest-leery, buddy-led, we centers turned edges   we shelters turned chutes

BLACK-FACED IMPALA

an extinction

Quoth Quorn: you roost, you rot, no nut, you,
no worst wurst, no hog guts, snouts.
Your runt joy un-hours, though
our own story grows. Our stunt gown turns
us to "hons'" (not Huns). You won't go on.
Our jury struts out, two north, two south,
two Johns. Though your honor won, you run.
Gusts tour your town, turn soy to rugs.
Truth: you sought *now*. You got *soon*.
Your own *no* hurts. Shoot, your worth grows horns
hunts shun. No toy guns shout, no not-toy guns
short sons or oust youth to urns.
Worn-out, your hurts nosh your sun.
Turn you un-on. Toons ruin your shows—
no Zorros, no thugs or goons. Who hunts who?
Who got got? To sort now your zoo.

MARGAY
an extinction

cold doles out icicles   who will joust with one?
cold itself will, I bet   independent of feud   though the sun
could hunt it   if not so listless behind clouds

       but, no   the sun's list includes:
locket of soil, tinsel of pine, soul's window open-shut-open-shut—
its zenith undoes the neck, unties then unites vision   up, up

so little depends upon   how the edifice is built
if the countdown continues   despite copious hiccups

    huddled up in the question, the indelible wound

WOOD STORK
an extinction

an aqua-haul　　　　　liminal animal

changing, fleeing—　　　　leaching a magma, a finale

albumin in camp aluminum　　　　an unappealing meal

fin-mail—fan-mail　　　　fallible chain mail　　　　hex-flinching

feeling quinine-beneficial, having acumen, un-fumble magic—

enable elegy by Heimliching even a bump-giving flea,

by failing

piece by piece, call up Pangaea—

a place again

amphibian, mammalian　　　　a family, finally

even familial baggage　　　　excellence in cheap blame

—a balm:

manna expunging famine

a minimum, heaping

ʻAkekeʻe

an extinction

conscious of nightly symbols forming on historic forts

    how to unfold   unmoor   unmission

to join   issuing forth your country into my country

so hot so unbound   not occupying but simply   touching

    my own tropic cools   this fusing isthmus shorts

                dibs on unwounding

    stop this posturing   this conviction disposition

thoroughly mining this bituminous night for lost hours

     dust-gluttonous   tumor-thorough

pumicing our moon's bright foot

     involving full-grown minors or mirrors in this whodunit

trying not to but noticing   this world's voluminous booty

     flossing with history's thong

    with history's wrongs   showing

monolithic thoughts build phobic logics

it's on us to unbuild

clog this porous wisdom

with your good or mostly good oil

LEMUR
an extinction

Thinking is a shanty boat I go onto
on this good Ohio night

What is "sight" to a window?
What is a window's fantasy?

Vision goofs—"saw" saws in two: what was wasn't

Is a scab cash that was a body's savings?

Is a body a ghost's citation?
A ghost's stowaway past?

Winnow this instant as if it is chaff

I saw a body that wasn't a body

a shopping bag posing as snow atop hay
a twin pawning a notion of two

In this invitational, a coast fights its sinking
Not a job I'd want

What widows a window? No gazing?
No noticing that goat, that hint of noon on that
happy stoop, that siphon in that gas tank,

that kind of aching hatching knowing is

MA'OMA'O
an extinction

edified by renewed cells   but, besides insides' surprise un-ruins,
terrible   utterly   delinquent relief   sulking
elsewhere   in reruns, we review Eden's western lung
wheezing, punctured by infinite suffering   this denuded
requiem   just ting beside ting   this single bell   stuffing its
gutted tin pelt   pretending this swinging pistil will still seed

FLYING FOX
an extinction

Bad press? Add ache. Deter meme-streak:
assure them, *we're death-mask empaths—just*
breeze-captured ash, steered here. See a TV? Act
mute. Erase a week? Act dazed. What address
redresses mar: madam, dear, the best? Here's
a muse-blast: we're cash at a web's cashed ATM,
ether that passes as earth's purr, a water-cat
dew made but heat ate. Cue the champs:
team teat. Makers, make eased the starved.

GORAL
an extinction

despite sci-fi's pessimism, we tune-up just fine, if finicky, system-wide

the new equipment mystifies us with its chic skin

we must buff   send up its denuded sheen

the subject's impediment is independence   seed-wishes—intents

        citizenship thickens us

          sediment in descent

    sentiment is niche   centipedes minus feet

        hundies in twenty tens

whimsy deceives   we must be punishment's students

bid by it   "induce quiddity   then snuff it"

CHINCHILLA
an extinction

error's robot wrote *body body body*
week to week   week or two of
better yogurt: pure fuss, gourmet sorrow

woke to "best of" of sex
yet   bored oyster   but
deeper fork worked
burst purse

gorge-just   murmur off your muumuu

suds grope form
soft dowry of regret

youth's porous detour   droop-troupe
dumb fumes

geese perk up sky

our seer borrows dust from dry streets
moved by go's story, our seer, too, goes

poster of empty eggs
poser vortex demoted to storm-sour gust
ego-stuffed motor ordered to zoom

joy stems from bye

red red ruses

OKAPI.
an extinction

Cud futures nurture; semen nurtures future; we rent
thus cede future returns; they lend fumbles (un-fun fees,
embedded); hymns crust muteness; few feud; burnt birch,
leggy hog, mere yes: where's the demented "between"?
They quest the ledge the sheen butters; they rend the curse

under heel, underwhelmed; nude trust breeds beech-esque
buttresses, lest we shun mess. Unwell, then well, then
under wellness. Mull here, my stunted mulberry,
my sun-rusted herd. He, she, they test need—jeer. West
be yet wester. Melt be yet wet's best verse: re-un- -er's -est.

DUGONG
an extinction

Here's a beast-less fable, a feckless tale, a sea sick with rhythm

A trawl's empire has twelve fish, excess shrimp, yesteryear's kelp palaces, plastics
as empires "have"   at the behest, at the helm

A machete clears

Here's a fable: all the beasts
keep their "all"   Malaise sets, celestial-like,
a hemisphere at a time

Time is feral after all   yet trackable

If a library is with bestiary as a wife is with babe
prepare a lap, alter a breast (altar it)

What lives is a liver: a part, a piece   a meerkat
that's a clapper   that strikes the mammal bell

BEARDED SEAL
an extinction

Though you jut, night-coin, hunky moon, in you go—thin

Who to un-tough tough with touch

Took to couch, took to cot   no Zion

No thing to chug topnotch hooch if fun ought hoof on in you

With thy ping-ponging opinion jump to who to mummify   how to zinc thy quick

Why notch if not to count   if not you too   counting

Touchy   touching iffy

No hymn to pithy noggin

"Foggy" thinking   nitpick picnic

You wing it   not with thy own wing, with wing of thy top minion

To unchink now thy mighty cup

AVAHI
an extinction

Roots offer credence   Rudder-esque, one's steered

  Seems you'd be better off booger   never nose

    Once broken   "just once" no true "just"

  One's brokenness endured   (you conjure now

two wedded scenes: letterpresses rejected by types, endlessly word-less,

  our self—Puget Sound's tumescent fogs   mere bulges

    no cotton boll moons to pluck) We go on our own

  Flummoxed, we wonder, "Were we?"   Yet we refuse

to open lockets offered to us   Our toe told our body: "Good lord,

  your gene pool's too cold to enjoy" We keep out (our self, ~~negated~~)

Kokako
an extinction

Triggered by winter's grunt—icy trees felled,
vehement winds—she flustered. Similes described her
such: deep plié, insecticide-bit chigger, melt-free butter,
scentless mint. She finds festivities, well, festive,
despite her mind teeming with unimpressed fish,
feeding in her river, if river is desire, unmet, untended.

*

If desire is distended, underfed, find it biscuits, sing it
beef-hymns, write it in with eggs, lichen it with gristle—clutch,
cling. The steeple isn't puncturing the blue, is it, but fingering it.
Let's let this feel "humming." Let's let this feel bicycle-light,
submerged in spring. The view is suede hillsides, cut by
mist, trimmed with the creek's help. Desire builds its victims.

*

Seething. Winter's been jilted by tulips. Duende mustn't
end. Similes' stunts trigger distrust. My big being is twinned:
fissure, pith. We flusters I. Hits slightness's nerve.
The timer lets up light, which gets feisty with the view. Preens.
The lithe verb bends the field, -ing-ing. Presents presents. Fleur-sure.
The turnip's triumph isn't being bitten, but being dirt's pulled hem.

DHOLE
an extinction

I'm just saying: acquit my gargantuan vacancy

making pain an aquarium

making immunity this sanctuary

giving a crack impunity

pitting sumac against spirit (stamping it)

A criticism is but a gust in a straw-stiff barn

a giving misgiving

a taxi taking its turn

My past is as an army is—away

a Spartan awaiting a sign

WOOD BISON
an extinction

Text a future female a lace hatchet,
fur à la carte, a pelt grave. The temper
part prayer, part leak, the purr all cave.
A plump hurt kept—a gruff meal.
Grace gave tact a lamp. The hurtle felt
my fault. Thump, thump, late heart.
Laugh a Greek laugh. Yelp my hug. Pray
the reef make, cheer the reef up. He may
mute a pager. Errata: He may mute me.

AVAHI
an extinction

Moon's tour of ponds reflects detours snow took

        young snow's ego-less melt

            To unbecome to become

Our ego's bordered by flowers slowest to boom

        Our egos—murky cocoons   respond to
mournful coups: *nest not* (*n'est* knots)

To be lemur-less, to be stunned—country-less globes
        bowls but no tongues, molested wool suddenly unmolested

           Beefless cow   cowers not, kowtows to seed

Perky from sleep, bounty's clone blesses bone

        Nude skeletons emerge, sun-meek, body-keen,

        monsoon-boosted, no skull-skulk—desert deserted by desertness

Strung pole to pole, our closest story   bound to weep dry

        Forests forget words, get lessons: *remember*
cruelty once took bloom *to be* fester *so left*   *fooled by concepts of* done

KOKAKO
an extinction

if we budget grief   if grief deputizes cynicism

did we invent yet the cipher we will need

we've underutilized difference

if we were just feeding-tube diligent

if we were pertinent wives   even just self's rhyme

illnesses meter the spine's neglected line   we slump inside the music

*

we let the erstwhile rift lessen   yet urge eiders' quibble

with Neptune   preferring his substitute in Greece

     with empire's whim, we turn

swift reviews suggest systemic repressive tendencies

we issue quizzes   require five similes refiguring dependence

if perfect, we permit thirst   we insist we'll even quench it   yet never yet did

Green Turtle
an extinction

I'm psychic   I say
Psychosis is a map's daddy   (oh how my id shows)
A spooky compass hijacks a map   so aid's amiss
I show chamois chamois   I show oaks a box of oak
(shock shook off whimsy)   Oak-mad, I ask: is FOMO a fad?
My ax asks: may I hack away? may I dam a maw(k)ish womb?
        (body as chasm   soma as chaff)
Doom is a sad comma   has a wish: *may my hook hook*
a vapid mass   a sick-ish pod   jizz's spam
If I avoid asps' jaws, wisdom-awash, I ask if I may
pass days off as sad food   (bad bash)

DUGONG
an extinction

appetite's hallmark: that they   *brim with*

    —*they?* .   a spherical *they*   heavy

typecast as all heave   ample aviaries yet tweet-less

     scratch that—appetite is faraway

we are they   a chia pet with a simple harvest

     the schism is effective   what we pick   what we trash   what we *we*

ersatz leashes fail like we fail   stray after stray

     better material perhaps will   reshape shame

we seek a preview   what a seer sees

     she says   wait as chai tea waits   the price is steep

the lake's they-face shimmers, its mask lifts   maybe if we master

     that lift?   —the spell affirms the caster

PANGOLIN
an extinction

Request the future be muted—de-futured, reef-esque

The myth remembers news, remembers truth, recedes

(ebb's best study)

Where the huckster's keyster thudded

bets were bet

Webs seemed rested tutus

seemed rebuked shutters

busy beds

FLYING FOX
an extinction

Ease craves abracadabra but that's rare.
Rare as map-true treasures. As mad campers.
As upchuck deemed "a beaut." Success makes us
seethe—Tupperware must just keep, whereas we
must be esteemed. A steam a steam a steam. (We steamed.
Teamed up.) The death we tempted rebuked us. The packrats
rejected us. Much was averted. Papers were persuaded: "repress
trees' pasts." A rebus was made: a pea, a cub, a puckered mouth.
Are we scared? Ha. Wash these sham scars.

MARGAY
an extinction

Which level of deceitful? Knock-off-
Louboutin-kitten-heels level? With kitten teeth
used to cobble the heel? Even novices know
to find online   skinned ocelot's pelts
no booth sells. To vend "the skin of teeth."
The zenith of "just sufficient." So close to not.
This closeness. This insistence. One's inflexible
question: life. We found ethics' fossil then sold it.
Left votive bills to billow in insidious winds.
The deciduous exit is kind of exodus.
No one coped. No one hiked deep in the bone.
How often the pond lets sinking be   itself.
How often we sunk. How often we didn't.

BLUE WHALE
an extinction

Props to visitors for not knocking mysticisms.
Conditioning is no picnic. I'd risk ignoring victory
if it got toxicity to stop. I'm stoic if my mirror's stoic
(not oft)—I mimic it, groping. My form is my commons.
Sick doctors trip, voicing, "Skin's minor koi pond stinks."
I'find synonyms for insisting, "I'm opposing!" Not condoning?
Moving into "no," "for good"? Skin is prison stock.
Proving sordid. Dirty coin. If I root my scion, forging spring?
My prognosis is off—I'm citing gods. I'm stooping.

BEARDED SEAL
an extinction

I hock out my puck moon—
it won't cotton to night. No point.
Too quick to go with common joy.
Too quick to go on with not knowing.
Too quick to go off in my Uffizi of fog
in which (on which)   thing upon vying thing
hung. I cough my gummy cough, cuing
nothing. On my own. Fitting in with
my finicky ovum. Fitting into it—
oh, wincing hutch. Chin up, my chick—my wing,
my thigh—I'm giving you my mouth-cot.

KUHL'S DEER
an extinction

Pac-Man voyaging point to point, not noticing
gnawing wiping away a gaming nation

To boot, a wingman of Pac-Man wanting topping off

Pac-Man can't go   amniotic—can't go
off again—an atomic bomb not an option

Pac-Man can act "in captivity" to zap copping to a fact:
Pac-Man won't "not"   piggy pig
iconic tomb-maw   a taxing yap

Pac-Man pivoting now to man

DHOLE
an extinction

a fungus spars in risk's ring, un-bats a cavity

rain pranks an ark, acts a mass unmaking
but is just a spit

an ark minus mating, a swung fist minus a jaw,
a fist-bump minus unity, an *ain't* minus a twang

my king ain't a crust a pizza wants back
my captain ain't purity's mutiny: gunk, mar, maim

ain't I aspic's sway, pig-bits, turnip-bits
in a mutant mitt

a gut's gimmick is in fact crap

art warns: fact is uncut grass that wants cutting

a wasp strung stings, trimming skin as if
Santa's just a gif away

maintain

brain's synaptic swag—a past it can pass back

GORAL
an extinction

It seems we despise us—it seems we must—(we mutts)—it seems
      we must even end—the theme "insufficient"—meet it—
        even the beehive needs henchmen

The scenic minus species—dust-ups mute them—mind, yes, mind—
      we mind   we thumb menus—vibe with tempeh, vibe
        with seed-cheese, dip chips in festive stuff

        my skin is inked, my skin is missive
        dismissed—my skin is hype
        when skinned

            beside me, a demented medic pumps
            inside me, a demented medic pumps
            hunky medicine   my type
                hi, cutie, meet up? me up, me
up, I'm up, I'm up

        cinched in me: *I*
        sunk in me: *I*
        my quick

          Bisquick-efficient *I*
            this species' cup

Speech-divested, defensive Twinkies fume behind the chimney they mimic
      (in extinct's vicinity   we sense
                    they just need pity)

Is "need" defective?
I sit, stumped by pine

I sit, pining

GIANT PANDA
an extinction

Chromosomes form self's reef—we reek of luck.
Shells overwhelm shore's bosom: less jewelry, more leech.
Overwhelm me, Yoko. Be my ovum's yolk.
My Elmer's flubs, fuses lobe & bulb, skull & bloom.
Messy crumb of us crumbles more. We're *else*.
Summer schemes brooks, muumuus, church of
mushrooms—morels. We seek some. We're our souls' humus,
yes? We observe lemurs floss creeks, loose
bush from rock. Reefer-less. Here, for you, four brews,
cheese, chemo for your cells, emo for your moors. Some hero.

WOOD BISON
an extinction

late luck let her level up   make empathy a career
after that came face-plumage   tear after tear (a tear-rally at a face)
      therapy a hatchery   a hem-met fray

they make the future haggle   a meeker (calmer?) future gave up
      get = have *v* get = leave   clearly a matter
        (later, they regret the term "value")

a hack: make up a fearful allergy   let them quell that fake ache,
let a heat lamp prepare a "fever"   cue the leech!
    fault me my early prayer: a "tame" earth, a muzzle, a lure

GREEN TURTLE
an extinction

Who am I boss of? My iPod? My pick?

I had him as a sow has ham

If I sob a swamp, if I'm hid by sob-camo
If a swamp is Camp Sob—a soppy wish

Hiss—how is my wish a wash, a soap sick of foam?
A hawk who hawks his doom?

Did I miss my sad hippo—a hammock of *if*?

Away, bossy iamb!—who dams my *said*, my *say*

Is *I* a happy scab? I spams my id-box

Bookish, Mom picks commas as if a posy
A posh dick sways
I mop piss, dish chic food, famish

A wasp picks my body as a so-so dock

I pass as da bomb's damp wick
I am my mask

TOTOABA
an extinction

Like nude milk's luminescence; like sky's fleece
sheep envy; like swim-shirked rivers, wending
like slurred cursive; like hymen-less frills; like
luckless messes; like greedy reminiscence—
here's duress; like plucky winds plucking up
pine, elm, spruce, hewn pieces; like purple's rhyme;
like hyphens' kin: reins, screws; like likenesses;
unlike furred cheese, unused; unlike Jung's sleep;
unlike pride's insides, pressurized; unlike
minus's plus side; unlike self versus
selflessness, in which self is like eggs, gulp-
wedded; unlike luckiness's guise—"uncursed";
unlike places where feeling reigns; unlike
skin-skilled silk, flesh slips up, plunders life's sense.

GRAY WOLF
an extinction

The kid executed his descent stint   then "did" time (sexed time up?)

The upside: he exhumed evidence his epic kin didn't mute
the muse   then substitute nimbuses' music

The muse just untied She-ness   un-chipped the pet Peeve
        quit   then edited the quiet   deepened it

Much debuted   Much—even "much-ness," un-excessive—teemed

The kid seized this   hunted the hush, didn't just beseech it
meet me, meet me, meet me (it didn't)—the kid bets, "next time" (dejected detective)

MANDRILL
an extinction

suppose we guess by cost who's to occupy those houses

we keep to hopscotch boxes, though eyes go out, covetous

the coup to bust up the techy web goes south—cue the test tube few vow to egg

success's photo op's just bosses, though ought be us, too

gesso wets the guest, but the guest botches the job, yet gets quotes

to buy, buy, buy, coos, "so bespoke," queues to see chests of sought coffee,

hutches of scotch—they suggest, "the hobby chooses you"

touché   toss up: exposes you best: the jukebox, the quest?

Lemur

an extinction

as antagonistic as a coast chastising sand   a habitat it can't kick

want sits   stoic   standoffish   —ha, as if

                                  wiggly want, sadistic want

      its own fiasco   want is a canyon not any boat can boat down

        stay back, zodiac   no signs   of   going okay

           an iconic agony—soapy as TV at noon

    as with an aging body   a coast's waist stops abiding its cinch

    wait   it is a body, isn't it?—navigating its own waning

        —to ossify   to ghost changing

as satisfying as fission striking a kinship with dyads—that division, too, can bond

GIANT PANDA
an extinction

echo's error's re-less

bubbles wobble, hover—sky-bushes, feeble couches for sky

hollow orbs   hell's mum vowels

bless clueless elk, moose, foxes   clueless yeses

here, blush blurbs our cheeks

flowers bluff   refuse bloom, refuse verbs

our work burrows   oeuvre-corks

sebum lurks below, mushroom-esque

ever more corks   close us

look how shook our heroes   our fever-surly cells

RED LECHWE
an extinction

in an imagist funk

ant on a sofa mistook as a mountain

big to it

baby possum atop a giant tomato

not a mom   ova it, so ova it

a puffin says, if a puffin says, *auks*

a nosy moon butting up against a gossipy sky

moaning on: *font isn't ink's outfit*

okay, okay

CHEETAH
an extinction

ominous door, missing doorknob   good squirm
        no *x* guns down *y*   I know loss's idiom

fumbling girl: moon-limb   idolizing puddling milk—
slimy rug   sloppy slip   slipping on

        no gown, no skull ring   I'd go for being
ivy bullying building's walls   I'd go for being

Ovid's vigorous word-body   unfolding, giving voids form
        sitting gods down   mudpuppy in mud, kingly minnows

my lord-gripping kinfolk   snub us   no sizing up
        or upsizing

your briny boys,   lungs, filling—
        donning wings of lung, un-ill, unknowing us

        numbing

        Our loop unloops

KOALA
an extinction

there's bushfire, then there's urgency
there're hints, then there's news
there's existence, then there're endings

the pier's wet peer might dry up, the inn might be
bed-free   this we pretend is fine
          just *is*   us, being

                    the Bitumen Queen teems in her pit—
she refunds the center with   the periphery
          See, this suits!   Rent these few mirth-drenched nights

Sidestep fuss with fizz   Cheers! (We even chipped in!)

BLACK-FACED IMPALA
an extinction

Our thorough host ought not
shun ghost tours or hurt ghosts.
Shrug not. You sworn to sow song not hush.
Tough hours. Thy thought-thong shows. Thy noon
runs to two. Turns out our runt story's
got guts. Gory roots. Youth sours us.
Who won Uno stung. Stow thy sting.
How you grunt. To roost now. To grow
non-rot suns. Why not honor
our wrongs?—go, "how just our hunts!"
Wow. Just wow. Truth—thy stout ox—tugs us.
Short sojourn. Town to town
to urn. "Too soon." Our own zoo ousts us.
Our own tooth on us nosh. Our own
worst sons turn us to johns. Go on. Go.
Not to strut now, tux snug. Not to swoon.

GIBBON
an extinction

dream up   *after*
dream *dread's dug-up acre*

a farmed heart   freed of tree-matter
    all that fell

         heap three, heap twelve

ump my lack
make the call

*

fear-caulked   hurt acted a crutch

that weep made a puffy jacket what we had
called a face

quarrel-laced allure   temper deferred

very adult—that clam-wet ache, that late datum

where a cell that had a healthy crew ruled

revelry actually a rematch   a daydream

      revery, a vacuum

PANGOLIN
an extinction

three servers query my druthers   my druthers, huh?

heck, serve us cucumbers   Tex-Mex zest   the secret reserves

surf my turf   butter my better stems

the system's buddy's severed   the best eke by, fettered by fees

terms restructure us
ever the tree, the desk's cred bests the seed's

we were excesses   stuffed dressers

bereft rescues, we wrested "deserve"

crested the berm
uttered "bummer" where streets were
subsumed by refuse

the set where we were embedded reset

"de-" rejected "struct"
"re-" secured fresh "members"

try here
the future's the referee

RED KNOT
an extinction

A fig is a basic blimp, limb-asail, up, up—
all champs slump, fall, as music may, if limp.
Imp, whip up magic: a mall's macaws mill,
bills full. Ship my bully away. Ship us.

Mush wigs a pig's maw. Such glam lips, as vamp
as mica a slab pimps. A law is ump, is lamp's
bulb-hush. Shhh. A paw as a cab a fish miscalls—
chum? Chums? A sup appalls. Simply a wall.

Us-ish, bubbly, a miasma claws. My mass
chills. I gasp. Baby says, chug, Valium will
slim my ails. Uphill, a film-clip calms. Him
claps. A happy lump. Musical-awash.

I gig, amass cash. I Bach, Bach, chic as
a lamb, casual as a quiz I smugly fail.

GRAY WOLF
an extinction

Citizen Suspect quiets the inquest
Despite "evidence," Citizen Suspect insists, "It isn't me"
(It *isn't* Citizen Suspect)
Citizen Suspect, supine, pines, keenness injected in stem
Citizen Suspect debunks the quiet kink hidden in the bunny's equipment
Citizen Suspect is steeped in minuses
Citizen Suspect deems justice quite behind
Citizen Suspect evinces, "It isn't me demented tides exist in"
Citizen Suspect buddies up—his puppet-stint
Citizen Suspect is the substitute's substitute
(Uh-huh, Citizen Suspect minds)
Citizen Suspect chimes in, "This cements it! I'm the victim!"
Citizen Suspect invites the pine scent in but evicts the pine
Citizen Suspect is evicted
Citizen Suspect thinks in snippets
Citizen Suspect bleeps citizenship's sickness but hunts its nixed bits

JUNE SUCKER
an extinction

a TV told
of a wall, a gloat

a body bid
that a moat halt
what might dim it—
to loot god
of doom—
a moot gig—a limo
with a flat—a lamp
lit at midday

RED LECHWE
an extinction

just as mutinous as off-intuition,

a pious motion—to not top sons—quieting gumption

bogus as insisting no toppings on a potato-you

to stoop, to saga   fasting nova, a gaunt moon

satisfying a faux-sky   —   atoning took all my savings

making a potion to stop a stumping toxin

a bonus: Saint Institution—a bastion, a mainstay—

making a baby of it, taking it in   naming it

(not just an atom's pain's a bomb)

KUHL'S DEER
an extinction

If fiction taint fact, if ammo cannot
if fact miff faction   woof

A wan tan I am not
Not a gig in a coffin, no toxic yawn

A maw in want of a wonton
A wig in want of a bang
A font too big to nix

Pant, baby   act minty, nomnom

I'm a pontoon in motion
I cannot fib or fawn, tagging town
my point in paint, my paint atop my pain

"Now, go"   my motto
          now winnow point to pint
to pot it   a paw of gin

in want of a tonic of cat   To go catatonic
gift man a common fiction: pomo poof
no *mot*—no mo'   woman, a gap   a comma

WOOD STORK
an extinction

a human-animal nagging a flame
        a human feeling all animal, feeling even fungal—capable, nimble,
                      menacing
a flame clubbing in a chimenea
        an emcee-flame, jump, jumping, maybe imbecilic, maybe amazing
a chimenea calling a chill a bluff
            having a final call, a late-given name
a bluff chiming in, "call me cliff"
        having a calling: hay, a bale; chimney, a fume-camp; a lumen, a lamp
an aching villain giving up evil
        a liminal man filing a manacle, a manacle hemming in a *my*,
            a manacle making an *I* an enemy
a belly-up evil balancing a blame-heavy heaven
        a feeble heaven bingeing un-healing, an un-cinema
a plunge mapping an icy blue
    piling life in, an *agua*-yenning mule, muling—mulling if meaning is all meaningful
a neap pumicing a beach
            a June beaching a May

JUNE SUCKER
an extinction

my ballad, a DIY jail   a habit to loofah away

go   foil my maw   that igloo

    got a whiff of a god   who'd had a pity body

                a moot womb

I'm told   that llama tattoo will molt   what of it

a data-lag will add to a doom motif   my pallid lamb, my blight

      flood of my pathway   I paid

   pivot   joy might fail   oh

that oddity   joy   oh, oh   I'm all jolt

   both/with   oh   my lax math will do

Ma'oma'o
an extinction

When inner sun is tested, when inner shield stutters null its heft

Under less stress, we've plunged

Feeling returning   girl-tusk un-hunted, guy-tusk hid in glens

If being were wilt-free, un-lettuce-like

Like lint in the belly's cubby, put there by in-ness   being *in*

Lint's heir is dust   ("us" is there, see?)

We're kinks in the field   Un-breed the bitterness

Un-christen luck   "blessed"

When thinking is blustery   wind inside, deluge   indigestible

gristle   Pitted, cherry-wise—fight-less yet the ruckus

wields us   Rewind, but   rewind

We've flunked the bees   let seep their tub—being's plug pulled

MUSK DEER
an extinction

If not annihilating pain, localizing it

a toxin not wholly a villain   nibbling away

bit to obit   what agitation

an optional twin   botching *only*   a placating caption

I   that loon   waving to a falcon

a conch with which to call   inviting in a pang

to low   oh, coping cow   what a vacation to go on

that way of a clot   with no nationality   finally clotting

MANDRILL
an extinction

CEO of *we*, post-*they* (how though?)
CEO of wee   joy's boss

the ghost uses the key fob to ghost *go*
          ghost got guts   ghost guts ego

                    the stuff of stuff

cobweb-stuck, cobweb-showy, fog-soft, hope copes—
          boycotts foe thoughts   two by two

guess who the guest quotes

                    the fussy buck peeks out of bush
     shoot   buck-speech *v* buckshot

                    punk   punctu—   stet

we covet gusto   shucks, we covet "get"

sweet sock hop bop, feet-fête, suppose they botch youth
               suppose we
                         botch

                              too busy to seethe

the test-house put out of house
　　　　bespoke coop, too creepy
　　　　　　ghost tock
　　tock tock　　　stoke the hush

　　ghost stock

soup of the us we oust　　　　(the chef upset

　　we woke)

　　　　shuck us
　　　　suck us out

CICEK
an extinction

extra as nouns' dramas that unfold

a sambal of shadows flavors a gallows' human haul

what word's yours?

say that   allow two sorrowful protons a solo pronoun

a porous room won't hoard   hands out drafts (not

draft as war's favor   but draft as door's sap)   not to patrol as a puma

fallow marsh   arduous growth

pay to pass glass that guards an ossuary that guards a body's flotsam

what for mastodons? shoot as many

photographs as shot of Portugal's famous tram   to that way hold

DIBATAG
an extinction

once we fell for "lemony freshness"

      smell enforces norms

preen now

skewer "so profesh"

      spunk—no recluse

lover of pores

open   open   preserve

eons' envelopes

frozen corpses—parcels of *once*

our cells our lockers we use for self's school

      no rescue for poor lessons

so numerous   our expenses

chrome only one

        we screens

RED KNOT
an extinction

achy music will amplify glacial mucus
        (ugly facial) (caul-ish)
a casual *if* will smugly sully *happily*
a family's gills will fail

why wail a Shamu-big wail?
as a basic law, claws will claw
always is a special balm (*always* a sham)

CICEK
an extinction

Sappy TV pulls an old hurt up   vast as lust

                   A phantom thaws

    Not as lazy as argon, that hurt lands a wallop and

    a trust rusts or bursts   all trust?   (*worry not*)

Past a mortuary, past a lush quad, a mortal stratum holds

          Froth of astral labor

Valorous lantanas grow
        and grow

    A sad frat slurs   sprays:
    DRUGS LAST PAST LUV

      "hurry   pass hash and stash that stuff,"
      an aura-proof human hums

      (Astral labor sounds an alarm at that lampoon)

      but what human's aura-proof?

Numb, a past wow now won't stun

Ash as party fur   as hurry's tomb

A summons looms

among savory growth youth affords

(a dollop of youth now to laugh at, lap up)

How to un-stump a stump, how to outlast a last straw

GAVIAL
an extinction

the courtroom rotted, unused   beyond, the under-burdened
moon   some probe   or modest despot   who wrote the poem of us

thrown off by extreme freshness   softened by the source's sweetness
we detoured our protest   seduced by the rumor of the sorcerer's prowess
          (he's been quoted before   deemed future's mother   or fosterer)

our own syrup kept us stuck   we're ensured: somewhere the rumpus ensues
          who mutes   the SOS?   (we brush   the poor job
off on   so-and-so   fussy weed)   remember storks?
the myth of them?   to be born! debt-free!

one's one won—the spot secured   how sturdy   the pew of you
          how roomy the dorm   when you conjure "eons from now,"
do you see   we droned on   or we nuked   or we just   stunned

CHINCHILLA
an extinction

Fess up re: your regrets—preempt reports of
your worst Everest, too steep for you

Segue to some story of power   expressed by broke geodes,
empty zeroes   fog doxxed by fudged memory
of rebuffed storms

Before rebuked, some words toured your poem

You got spooked by fever promoted to embers
ousted from your form   to smote
      Rest up   so used to dew's effort-free wet
oh, to be doused   or for your deep to be dredged

BLUE WHALE
an extinction

Coming to roost, rinsing off my rind, my god-stint stops.
I did not mint ponds' fists
of cod, nor proof storm's porn of pink sky
or doom's sordid diction.
I go on typing my minor story/song on top of moon's ink,
forgiving "moving on" for not. My dominion fits my mood.
My domino stood in its rinky-dink portion
pining for its domino-kin.
Its void is my void.

Acknowledgments & Notes

The U.S. Fish & Wildlife Services' Environmental Conservation Online System served as the source for the endangered and threatened species featured throughout.

Thank you to the editors of the following journals, where poems from *Goners* first appeared:

Another Chicago Magazine: "Dugong" and "Ma'oam'o"
Bear Review: "Lemur" and "Red Lechwe"
Blood Orange Review: "Cicek" and "June Sucker"
Denver Quarterly: "'Akeke'e" and "Musk Deer"
DIAGRAM: "Black-faced Impala"
Echoverse: "Green Turtle," "Kokako," and "Mandrill"
Fonograf Editions: "'Akeke'e" and "Dibatag"
The Georgia Review: "Gavial," "Kuhl's Deer," and "Margay"
The Gravity of the Thing: "Flying Fox"
Jet Fuel Review: "Chinchilla," "Cui-ui," and "June Sucker"
La Vague: "Dibatag," "Koala," "Pangolin," and "Serow"
The Maynard: "Okapi" and "Wood Bison"
Nixes Mate: "Goral" and "Serow"
Pleiades: "Blue Whale," "Okapi," and "Wood Bison"
Poet Lore: "Chinchilla" and "Totoaba"
Posit: "Avahi," "Giant Panda," and "Green Turtle"
Puerto del Sol: "Cui-ui"
Storm Cellar: "Totoaba"
Tupelo Quarterly: "Black-faced Impala," "Cheetah," and "Flying Fox"
Under a Warm Green Linden: "Cheetah" and "Gibbon"

These poems were fed by these indispensable works: Lauren Berlant's *Cruel Optimism*, Inger Christensen's *Alphabet* (trans. Susanne Nied), Erika Cudworth's *Developing Ecofeminist*

Theory: the Complexity of Difference (especially her update of speciesism with the term and concept of anthroparchy), Forrest Gander and John Kinsella's *Redstart: An Ecological Poetics*, Jorie Graham's *Sea Change*, Matthew Griffith's *The New Poetics of Climate Change*, Donna Haraway's *Staying with the Trouble*, Elizabeth Kolbert's *The Sixth Extinction*, Denise Levertov's "Some Notes on Organic Form," Anna Lowenhaupt Tsing's *The Mushroom at the End of the World*, Margaret Ronda's *Remainders*, and Deke Weaver's *Unreliable Bestiary*.

Thank you to Chris Nelson and Green Linden Press for recognizing something in these poems and for giving the manuscript a home. Thank you to the Kentucky Foundation for Women, the Commonwealth Center for the Humanities and Society, the DISQUIET International Literary Program, and the University of Louisville English Department for grants, scholarships, and research money to develop this project.

I am deeply grateful to the numerous and generous readings the Sublimity City poetry group gave to these poems—thank you, V. Joshua Adams, Emma Aprile, Ann DeVilbiss, Kristina Erny, Jessica Farquhar, Danielle Fleming, Parker Hobson, John James, Kristen Miller, Juan Eugenio Ramirez, Ken Walker, and Kate Welsh. For nourishing friendship and bolstering during the writing of this book, thank you, Fran Freedman.

For compositional companionship, love to Gerty and Tang. For seeing me through the doubts and celebrating with me the triumphs, love and gratitude, Perry Sanders.

BIOGRAPHY

Kristi Maxwell is the author of eight books of poems, including *Goners* (Green Linden Press, 2023), winner of the Wishing Jewel Prize; *My My* (Saturnalia Books, 2020); *Realm Sixty-four* (Ahsahta Press, 2008), editor's choice for the Sawtooth Poetry Prize and finalist for the National Poetry Series; and *Hush Sessions* (Saturnalia, 2009), editor's choice for the Saturnalia Books Poetry Prize. She's an associate professor of English at the University of Louisville. Kristi holds a PhD in Literature & Creative Writing from the University of Cincinnati and an MFA in Poetry from the University of Arizona.

Colophon

For *Goners,* Kristi Maxwell is the recipient of the 2023 Wishing Jewel Prize, awarded annually for a manuscript that challenges expectations of what a book of poems can be. Named for an essay in Anne Carson's *Plainwater,* the Prize champions work that questions the boundaries of genre, form, or mode while engaging the rich possibilities of lyrical expression. Other titles in this series are available from Green Linden Press and Small Press Distribution:

- *schema geometrica* by Dennis Hinrichsen
- *You Would Say That* by Robin Tomens
- *Lunette* by Bruce Bond & Walter Cochran-Bond